The Essential 99 Punctuation Rules for Court Reporters

Workbook

Kenneth A. Wick

The Essential 99 Punctuation Rules
for Court Reporters: Workbook
(July 2020 Revision)

Table of Contents

Introduction

This workbook contains punctuation exercises for *The Essential 99 Punctuation Rules for Court Reporters* (Student Edition, Reference Edition, or video series).

It is not possible for a student to master punctuation by simply reading a textbook. Practice is necessary. The student's goal should be to learn the punctuation rules in the textbook and then practice the rules in the workbook. This way the rules become ingrained.

The exercises were developed and arranged to follow the progression of *The Essential 99 Punctuation Rules for Court Reporters*. There are 375 exercises that are punctuation specific (comma, semicolon, colon, etc.) and focus on one or more of the textbook rules. There are 125 "general" exercises that randomly cover all the textbook punctuation rules.

Abbreviations:
The below abbreviations are used within the workbook answers.

BGGP	*Court Reporting: Bad Grammar Good Punctuation* (2011. Sixth Printing, March 2016)
GRM	*The Gregg Reference Manual* (11th Edition, 2011)
LMEG	*Morson's English Guide for Court Reports* (Second Edition, 1997. Fourth Printing, January 2002)
MW	*Merriam-Webster.com Dictionary* (Approximately 240,000 entries. Accessed November 2018.)

The workbook is dedicated to my wife, Ellie.

This page is blank.

Grammar

Identifying Independent and Dependent Clauses
Exercises for Rules G3 to G5.

Place parentheses, ( ), around an independent clause and brackets, [ ], around a dependent clause.

1. Everyone was busy, and I went to the movie alone.
2. I will see if the book has arrived.
3. Mary needs to check back tomorrow before the store opens.
4. I'm counting calories, but I really want dessert.
5. Cats are good pets because they are clean.
6. Tommy dragged a chair across the floor while his mother watched in horror.
7. Tommy, who is 9 years old, was scolded by his mother.
8. The mistake which you made will be corrected.
9. I don't know where the keys are.
10. Her mom was pleased when she got the job.
11. As you read the textbook, you will find the answers that you are looking for.
12. He ran out of money, yet he didn't stop playing poker.
13. I drove to school with a friend.
14. I dove my car that recently got new brakes.
15. I do not know how far it is to school.
16. Mary lives one floor above you.
17. Our secretary, who is never late, called in sick at 9:00 a.m.
18. I do not know who gave her the flu.
19. The client said that he would call us next week.
20. When he calls, tell him our rates have slightly increased.

Identifying Conjunctions and Transitional Expressions
Exercises for Rules G6 to G7-1.

Place parentheses, ( ), around a coordinating conjunction and brackets, [ ], around a conjunctive adverb, transitional expression, or parenthetical expression.

21. Everyone was busy, and I went to the movie alone.
22. Sally didn't want to go to the dentist; therefore, he canceled.

3

23. He ran out of money, yet he didn't stop playing poker.
24. I lost my job. Consequently, my car got repossessed.
25. I left 30 minutes early; however, an accident still made me late.
26. To tell you the truth, I hate Monday mornings.
27. I saw the suspect. In fact, I can recall what he was wearing.

Identifying Prepositional and Verbal Phrases
Exercises for Rules G8 and G9.

Place parentheses, ( ), around a prepositional phrase and brackets, [ ], around a verbal phrase.

28. Don't step on the broken glass.
29. Seeing his excellent test score, he fainted.
30. The dog jump in the car.
31. The book on the table is now missing.
32. To provide a safe work environment, security cameras were installed.
33. Robert lives in the apartment around the corner.
34. Strong-minded to get the cookies on top of the refrigerator, Tommy dragged a chair across the floor.

Determining Essential and Nonessential Elements
Exercises for Rules G10 and G11.

Place parentheses, ( ), around an essential element and brackets, [ ], around a nonessential element. Insert commas if necessary.

35. A man who wore black is the suspect.
36. Brandon who wore black is the suspect.
37. The officer arrived in a black and white car a patrol car.
38. The defendant Mr. Smith hired a private attorney.
39. A psychologist Dr. Cooper is highly respected.
40. Amber's psychologist Dr. Cooper is highly respected.

The Period

Exercises for Rules 1 and 2.

Properly place the period. Capitalize the following word if necessary.

41. I passed the test
42. I passed the test we went out to dinner
43. Please speak up
44. Can you state and spell your full name for the record
45. I object the question is beyond the scope
46. Objection the question is vague
47. Objection ambiguous compound
48. Hurry we're going to be late
49. Damn I don't know okay
50. All right we can take a recess now

The Comma

Compound Sentences
Exercises for Rule 3.

Properly place the comma.

51. I'm counting calories but I really want dessert.
52. Everyone was busy and I went to the movie alone.
53. He ran out of money yet he didn't stop playing poker.
54. He said he was not in town yesterday but many people saw him.
55. Linda was telling the truth or she was telling a huge lie.
56. I lost my job last week and my car was repossessed.
57. Tammy could not decide what to do so she slept on it.
58. John didn't want to go to the dentist but he went anyway.
59. I only had eight reporting jobs last month yet I was able to pay the rent.
60. You should tell the whole story or you will face the consequences.

Introductory Clauses
Exercises for Rules 4 to 7.

Properly place the comma.

61. To provide a safe work environment security cameras were installed.
62. On reaching Nevada we stopped at the first place we could gamble.
63. Running out of money he didn't stop playing poker.
64. On the concrete sidewalk our dog obediently sat.
65. To tell you the truth I hate Monday mornings.
66. Across the street a squirrel darted with a nut.
67. Because they are clean cats are good pets.
68. In 2018 91 people graduated from the small elementary school.
69. He said he was not in town yesterday. However many people saw him.
70. While his mother watched in horror Tommy dragged a chair across the floor.

Nonessential Elements
Exercises for Rules 8, 9, and 11.

Properly place the comma.

71. He said he was not in town yesterday. Many people however saw him.
72. Mary Sue who is my half sister was born in 1984.
73. Did Dr. Smith your primary care physician see you last week?
74. I upon arriving at the accident scene fainted at the sight of blood.
75. It happened you know right after like dinner.
76. The tree tall and strong withstood the strong winds.
77. The motion filed just yesterday was immediately denied by the judge.
78. I don't' like the looks of this to tell you the truth.
79. Dr. Jones of WeCare Health is my physical therapist.
80. My situation in so many words is bad.

Series of Items
Exercises for Rules 14 and 14-1.

Properly place the comma.

81. I need to buy milk and bread.
82. I need to buy milk eggs and bread.
83. I need to buy milk eggs bread.
84. I need to buy milk and eggs and bread.
85. Please invite John Sue Jill and Sarah to the meeting
86. A court reporting student needs a steno machine a computer the textbooks et cetera.
87. A court reporting student needs to buy the textbook the workbook a notebook et cetera before the first day of instruction.
88. Did you mail the invitations and response cards and directions to the guests?
89. Did you mail the invitations response cards and directions to the guests?
90. Did you mail the invitations response cards et cetera to the guests?

Coordinate Adjectives
Exercises for Rule 15.

Properly place the comma.

91. It will be another hot windy day.
92. His cruel callous actions demanded a severe sentence.
93. The old ghost town is not on the map.
94. The smart charismatic employee quickly promoted to shift manager.

Miscellaneous
Exercises for Rules 10, 13, 16, 16-1, and 17.

Properly place the comma.

95. Please approach the bench Ms. Anderson.
96. I briskly walk never jog one hour each day.
97. Did you invite Melody Jones Esq. to the briefing?
98. Mr. Davies Jr. is also attending the briefing.
99. Explain what you mean sir by "gently used"?
100. The policy in question is Section 4 paragraph 12.

101. The attorneys conferred off the record not on the record.
102. Mr. Jones III died last week after a long illness.
103. Did you know Mr. Jones Sr. founded the law firm?
104. I am quoting from page 103 line 9.
105. Please speak up sir.

The Semicolon

Compound Sentences
Exercises for Rule 12 and Rules 19 to 21.

Properly place the semicolon and, if necessary, the associated comma. Do not separate independent clauses with a period.

106. My father's ancestors are from Germany my mother's ancestors are from England.
107. I saw James in the corner of my eye unfortunately I did not see which direction he went.
108. I did my homework however I did the wrong set of problems.
109. Ashley was the only person who could make the decision therefore she weighed the evidence carefully.
110. She weighed the evidence as a result the decision was sound.
111. Please schedule the deposition for Monday or if you prefer we can do it Tuesday.
112. Richard does not like broccoli in other words he hates it.
113. Her daughter loves broccoli and if you can believe this she asks for more.
114. I told the truth as I see it I told the whole truth.
115. I like him to be honest I love him.
116. I scheduled the car repair for this afternoon or in the event you're unavailable I can reschedule for another day.
117. I saw the accident my husband saw nothing.
118. I saw the accident needless to say my husband saw nothing.
119. I saw James in the corner of my eye thus I did not see which direction he went.
120. I saw James in the corner of my eye notwithstanding I did not see which direction he went.
121. I saw James in the corner of my eye and as a result I did not see which direction he went.

122. Jack loves Melissa in fact he sent her flowers.
123. Jack sent Melissa flowers obviously he loves her.
124. Jack sent Melissa flowers hence he loves her.
125. Jack sent Melissa flowers however he forgot the card.

Series of Items
Exercises for Rule 22.

Properly place semicolons or replace commas with semicolons.

126. Please grab the red ring of keys, the car keys, a bottle of water from the refrigerator, and my lunch.
127. I arrived at work at 9:30 a.m., turned on my computer, and called Denise, the director's secretary.
128. The defendant has lived in New York City, New York, San Francisco, California, and Detroit, Michigan.
129. The reasons for the employment termination were, first, excessive tardiness, second, substandard work quality, and, third, arguing with other employees.
130. I invited Jim, the office manager, Joan, the financial manager, and Linda, the supervisor, to the annual budget meeting.
131. The officer stated that he contacted the people living at the address of the complaint given five minutes earlier by dispatch that he talked to the people living at the address about the recent noise complaint of the party and that he advised the people living at the address to turn down the volume on the large stereo system.
132. My next available times are Wednesday, 9:00 a.m., Thursday, 1:30 p.m., and Friday, 10:30 a.m.
133. I quit my last job because, one, the manager was verbally abusive, two, better pay, and, three, better benefits.
134. The account payments were received on June 9, 2017, July 11, 2017, August 6, 2017, and September 10, 2017.
135. I consulted with my lawyer, Ms. Anderson, my CPA, Mr. Smith, and an expert in the field, Ms. Cooper.

The Colon

Exercises for Rules 23 to 25.

Properly place the colon. Capitalize if necessary.

136. Luke did not know a new law all bicyclists must wear helmets.
137. Amy is only afraid of one bug spiders.
138. He had his favorite meal when dining out soup, steak, and French fries.
139. The following law enforcement agencies were at the scene of the accident a sheriff, an NYPD officer, and a detective.
140. The accident report contained one glaring fact he was traveling well above the speed limit based on the skid marks.
141. An attorney advised me about my claim there was probably not enough evidence to win in court.
142. THE COURT Juror No. 5 is dismissed.
143. Susan passed the skills test her endless hours of practice paid off.
144. These are the reasons for the increase in Bay Area home sales economic recovery and low-interest rates.
145. I want you to understand that I saw a large, hairy thing that night a Bigfoot.
146. Several vehicles were involved in the accident a passenger car, a semi, and a pickup truck.
147. MRS. ANDERSON The witness has not been qualified as an expert.
148. John failed to make the job candidate list he was just shy of the experience requirement.
149. She had only one thought on her mind after rushing to get ready for work did she turn the iron off?
150. We know your reason for the murder money.

The Dash

Exercises for Rules 26 to 28.

Properly place the Dash.

151. I took borrowed the money.
152. I'll be frank with you mark my words because this is the honest truth I did not steal the money.

153. Q Did you steal
    A No.
    Q the money?
154. Q How long did it take you to recover
    A Four months.
    Q from the surgery?
155. The primary defense team Tom, Sue, and I was retained on April 2, 2018.
156. The needed food bread, milk, and cheese was bought on the way home.
157. Tom, Sue, and I the primary defense team was retained on April 2, 2018.
158. Bread, milk, and cheese the needed food was bought on the way home.
159. Q Were you speeding
    A Can we take a break?
    Q After this question. at the time of the accident?
160. Jackie, James, and Joan each will be speaking at the annual company dinner.

The Question Mark

Echo and Non-Echo Questions
Exercises for Rules 29 to 32.

Properly place the appropriate missing punctuation. Capitalize if necessary.

161. She's right isn't she?
162. He proposed to you Saturday evening didn't he?
163. There were two suspects wasn't there in the vehicle?
164. The children were excited were they not that Christmas morning?
165. You were headed southbound is that correct during the evening commute?
166. There were two suspects wasn't there to your knowledge in the vehicle?
167. You were headed southbound is that a good statement?
168. The defendant wore a blue jacket do you recall?
169. You were headed southbound isn't that correct?
170. She drove didn't she southbound?
171. You have never lived in a big city have you?

172. I'm right am I not that you've only lived out in the country?
173. You have only lived out in the country right?
174. You were headed southbound do you remember?

Questions with "To Be" and Connected Questions
Exercises for Rules 33 and 34.

Properly place the appropriate missing punctuation. Capitalize if necessary.

175. What I asked was did you date the plaintiff in 2017?
176. The question is why not?
177. Was his coat red white blue?
178. The question is this how is your father doing after his hip replacement?
179. What I asked was how much?
180. My last question was you saw Dr. Cooper on January 11, 2018?

The Quotation Mark and Italics

Punctuation Marks
Exercises for Rules 39 and 40.

Correct, if necessary, the period, comma, semicolon, or colon.

181. Freddie screamed, "fire".
182. "Let's go out for dinner", Rory said.
183. Linda turned the TV to a "nature show:" a shark feeding frenzy.
184. Tom said, "grab one;" "grab what", Mindy responded.
185. Susan asked, "Are you feeling lucky today"?
186. "I'm flying to Detroit", Tom signed. "You go where the work is".

Direct Quotations
Exercises for Rules 35 to 38.

Properly place quotation marks and other missing punctuation. Capitalize if necessary.

187. The officer said drop it.
188. She replied I'm going to quit this job if I don't get a raise.
189. James said I'll drop it off on my way home.

190. Put your hands on your head the officer instructed.
191. I got the job I squealed
192. The report says at 3:17 p.m., a stolen-car call was received.
193. The code section states all persons shall give a notice of 30 days.
194. Don't hit your brother Tammy said sternly. You must learn to share.
195. I'm going to quit this job she replied if I don't get a raise.
196. Rachel asked what do you want for dinner tonight?
197. Did Rachel ask what do you want for dinner tonight?
198. Did Angela say I'm making spaghetti for dinner?
199. The officer said quote drop it unquote.
200. William replied quote/unquote I quit.
201. The code section states quote all persons shall give a notice of 30 days.
202. The report stated the important detail on page 3 at 3:17 p.m., a stolen-car call was received.
203. The officer was forceful in his instructions drop it.
204. Peter said I don't understand these detailed instructions.
205. Amy responded I know the laws in this state.
206. I could not tell you Tim responded what Andrew's problem is.
207. The tax on the car is over $3,000 Randy gasped.
208. I think the suspect said quote give me your wallet close quote.
209. Did the suspect say quote/unquote give me your wallet?
210. Deborah asked how much did it cost to fix the car?

Titles, Special Emphasis, and Definitions
Exercises for Rules 41 to 43, 45, and 46.

Properly place quotation marks and/or use italics.

211. The book chapter is titled Know Your Punctuation.
212. Ann's favorite Home and Garden TV show episode is Backyard Décor.
213. Due to Jack's previous jail escape, he is termed high risk.
214. Mr. Wright said he bought a chopper, a gun, while on parole.
215. In Roberts v. Pharmco, the plaintiff claimed fraud.

216. Have you seen the Star Trek episode The Enemy Within?
217. What did Mr. Smith, the defendant, mean by self-help?
218. For your question, I recommend reading the chapter titled The New You in the bestseller Be Your Best.
219. The movie accurately captured the zeitgeist of the late 1970s.
220. The dictionary defines zeitgeist as the general intellectual, moral, and cultural climate of an era.

Capitalization
Exercises for Rules 50 to 59.

Properly capitalize each sentence.

221. ward stone ireland invented the stenotype.
222. main street and first street do not intersect.
223. have you read *the history of court reporting in the 1970s*?
224. did i leave my copy of *punctuation for proofreaders* on the table?
225. did you see captain james roller at the VFW meeting?
226. did james roller, captain of the 103rd infantry division, attend the VFW meeting?
227. ted cruz, senator from texas, attended the heated public hearing?
228. did you visit your mom during christmas vacation?
229. i can't believe dad said he was not coming for easter dinner.
230. is it true, detective, that you found a bloody knife in the trash?
231. the officer pursued the suspect's car south on elm street.
232. that's a distinctive accent. were you born in the south?
233. yes, i was born in new orleans near the french quarter.
234. the golden gate bridge is in the bay area.
235. the empire state building is in the big apple.
236. the headquarters of intel is in silicon valley.
237. the hoover city council meets wednesdays.
238. i live in the city of sacramento.
239. i got a parking ticket from the city of sacramento.
240. last june, i filed a claim in hoover county superior court.
241. eve filed a court case that summer.
242. the best time to buy a toyota prius is in january.

243. the worst time to buy a dodge truck is in july.
244. is tylenol or ibuprofen better for a toothache?
245. i lived with a roommate who insisted on using charmin toilet paper.
246. does new year's eve fall on a wednesday or thursday this year?
247. does the defendant understand english or spanish?
248. the suspect was described as either hispanic or caucasian.
249. the victim was sitting on a park bench reading the qur'an.
250. the victim is an atheist and does not believe in a god.

Numbers

Writing Numbers and Figures
Exercises for Rules 60 to 63.

Properly write or correct the number format (spell out or use figures) in each sentence.

251. I only have three pairs of tennis shoes.
252. I have over one hundred books in my personal library.
253. Was Linda eight years old when her parents divorced?
254. Amanda owns fourteen vintage cars.
255. Do you really own eleven dogs and two cats?
256. No, I two dogs and nine cats.
257. The population in Oregon in 1973 was 2,200,000.
258. Is the 1973 Oregon population found on page 1,103 of the transcript?
259. The U.S. national debt is expected to exceed $24,000,000,000,000 this year.
260. Is the city project estimated at $775,000 or $1.1 million?
261. Three squirrels ran across the road
262. 25 out of the 4500 ballots were received.
263. Two hundred three small earthquakes were recorded in California last year.
264. One hundred nine new bird species were cataloged in the last twelve years.
265. One-U is the apartment number.

Time and Dates
Exercises for Rules 64 to 66.

Properly write or correct the time and/or date format in each sentence.

266. The accident occurred on June 5 2016.
267. Did the accident occur on five June 2016?
268. Sue's birthday is August twenty-three 1995.
269. Her younger brother's birthday is October 11 1998.
270. The accident occurred on June 5 2016 along Hillsdale Drive.
271. The accident occurred on five June 2016 along Hillsdale Drive
272. The accident occurred in June 2016 along Hillsdale Drive.

273. I left work at five pm.
274. I left work at seventeen hundred hours.
275. I set my alarm clock for six fifteen.
276. I set my alarm clock for zero six hundred hours.
277. The morning commute traffic starts at 6 o'clock.
278. I leave for work at five o'clock when it's still dark.
279. The accident occurred on June 5 2016 at about seven thirty in the morning.
280. The accident occurred in June 2016 at about seven o'clock in the morning.

Money
Exercises for Rule 67.

Properly write or correct the monetary format in each sentence.

281. The car repair bill totaled about six hundred dollars.
282. Wow, I only paid four hundred fifty dollars for the same repair at my shop.
283. Did Amy give you a twenty dollar bill?
284. No, Amy handed me ten dollars and twenty-five cents.
285. What happened to the other seventy-five cents?
286. She bought a candy bar for seventy-five cents and gave me ten dollars and twenty-five cents.
287. Did Tim buy that motorcycle for ten thousand dollars?
288. No, he bought it for eight thousand.
289. What did Tim do with the spare two thousand dollars?

290. He purchased new tires for three hundred or four hundred dollars.
291. Tim also repaid his mom two hundred dollars.
292. For every returned check, there is a twenty-nine dollar and ninety-five cent fee.
293. Did you see the soup on sale for ninety-nine cents each?
294. Yes, that's a savings of about one dollar and fifty cents each.
295. Buy a dozen and save eighteen dollars.

Miscellaneous
Exercises for Rules 68 to 75.

Properly write or correct the number format (spell out or use figures) in each sentence.

296. My mailing address is 1313 Fifty-Fifth Avenue Woodside California 94062.
297. My previous address was 1 Mills Street.
298. I bought eight acres of my parents' property or 10% of what they own.
299. My height is six feet two inches; my brother is six three.
300. The new law needs a two thirds majority to pass.
301. Five eighths of students need financial aid.
302. The cut was three thirty-seconds of an inch deep.
303. The manufacturing process is described on page twenty-three, figure two.
304. The second step in the chemistry experiment is to add .3 ounces of water.
305. I was born in the 1990's.

Abbreviation
Exercises for Rules 76 to 78.

Properly write the abbreviations in each sentence.

306. The us national debt per taxpayer is $180,000.
307. The Greek Battle of Marathon occurred in 490 bc.
308. Is it true, doctor Cooper, that you failed to perform a complete examination?
309. How many local ceo's attended the city budget meeting?
310. Doctor Bell, dds, has been my dentist for nearly 20 years.
311. The report states, "approximate vehicle speed: 45 MPH"

312. Ms. Anderson, ceo, married Mr. Smith Sr., ph.d.
313. How many tv's do you have in your home?
314. OK. Did you steal the money, jewelry, etc.?
315. I told the 911 operator to come asap.

Apostrophe
Exercises for Rules 79 to 84.

Properly write or correct the apostrophe in each sentence.

316. Someone stole the plaintiffs purse from the courtroom.
317. Tom claimed the heavy lifting violated workers rights.
318. Aprils wallet is missing. Have you seen it?
319. Childrens toys are so expensive.
320. Franks testimony did not help the case.
321. I want to hear the next two witnesses testimony.
322. I bought some fresh produce at the farmers market.
323. How do you think the girls soccer team will do this year?
324. Don't use the boys restroom by mistake.
325. Is there one or two ls in traveled?
326. Each judge has their dos and donts
327. I spell my name, Bret, with one t, not two ts.
328. I sold my 68 Ford Mustang.
329. I don't recall. My last surgery was in either 2017 or 18.
330. Did you say "talkin" or "walkin"?
331. Cindy xed out the spelling mistake and wrote the correction above.
332. Patrick IDed the suspect who was handcuffed in the patrol car.
333. I 86ed the junk straight into the trashcan.
334. I need to get my boss's approval.
335. I gave my two weeks notice at work.

The Hyphen

The Hyphen
Exercises for Rules 85 to 89.

Properly use the hyphen in each sentence.

336. Who won the county wide race in district 2?
337. Were there any post operative complications?
338. The illegal firearms found in the raid consisted mostly of semi-automatic rifles.
339. The witness corrected his statement and remarked the exhibit.
340. I lived on a small coop until 14 years old.
341. Do you have and post Thanksgiving traditions?
342. Is your position at the law firm fulltime or part time?
343. The x ray technician x rayed my arm in four different angles or positions.
344. I invest in both long and short-term securities.
345. On Tuesdays, the board has an open and closed-door session.
346. Focus groups were divided into 20, 30, and 40-year-olds.
347. As I recall, I had a hotel room on the twenty-second or third floor.
348. My last name is Schmidt S c h m i d t, not Smith.
349. My name is Staci Green S t a c i G r, double, e n.

Compound Words
Exercises for Rules 90 to 93.

Properly use compound words and/or the hyphen in each sentence.

350. I once saw a group of zookeepers capture a man eating alligator.
351. The required typing exam for the job was a pass fail test.
352. Are there any cross references for the compound adjective rules in the *Chicago Manual of Style*?
353. Please check the time table to see what time the bus arrives.
354. I was short changed by the cashier.
355. Did you have your suit dry cleaned before the start of the trial?

356. A high level meeting was scheduled after the annual budget was not approved.
357. I feared a worst case situation: layoffs.
358. However, the bottom line results were no raises or overtime.
359. This caused a year of penny pinching purchases and decisions.
360. I hope the budget crisis is not a long lasting problem.
361. What stopped me cold was the are you seriously that freaking stupid look.
362. The fast paced and lopsided football game ended in our favor.
363. The newly formed football team needed more practice.
364. I received a how you doing after all these years? welcome.
365. The old coal mining town is a popular hiking destination.

Yes and No
Exercises for Rules 98 to 99.

Properly write the comma or period with *yes* and *no*. Capitalize if necessary.

Do you work for the San Jose Police Department?
366. Yes I do.
367. I do not no.
368. I work for the County of Santa Clara no.

Did you see Jenny leave the office that day?
369. Yes she left with James around 4:30 p.m.
370. I worked until 5:00 p.m. that day no.
371. No I did not see her leave.

Where you speeding at the time of the accident?
372. No I was not speeding.
373. No I was driving about 35 miles per hour.
374. The posted speed limit is 35 no.
375. No I wasn't.

General Practice

General Practice 1
Properly punctuate each sentence.

376. Logan suddenly left his job because one poor pay two poor management and three long commute.
377. I left my trash cans out too long and got a fifty dollar fine from the city of burlingame.
378. Isabella passed the final speed test she and her boy friend went out to dinner.
379. I saw the car in the corner of my eye at the last second unfortunately I was unable to avoid the collision.
380. Did Liam ask what shall we do tonight for dinner?
381. The suspect in the police line up was id-ed by Emma.
382. The crack in the wind shield measured seven-sixteenths of an inch across.
383. According to our records the date of loss is september five 2018.
384. The detained teens included a thirteen, fifteen, and seventeen year old.
385. I can't believe Jackson likes cooked carrots and if you can believe this he also likes other vegetables.
386. Sophia was tardy wasn't she to the best of your knowledge to work each day?
387. Punctuation mastery is a life long journey.
388. My mother called my about the situation, the water heater stopped working and there is no hot water.
389. Did mister pearson file a claim in lake county superior court?
390. Did you sell your classic 57 chevy at the car auction in may 2017?
391. I took aspirin for my headache isn't tylenol better?
392. The probation officer reported that he contacted a male and female living at the recently added address in the old case file that the couple stated they are renters who had moved into the home in either june or july of 2018 and that James had not stopped by to see them or been seen in the area for a long time.
393. The poorly constructed wood deck cost me five thousand dollars to remove and rebuild.

394. I bought several tomato sauce cans for sixty cents each and saved two dollars.
395. Riley Walker lieutenant in the salvation army helped organize the winter clothing drive.
396. Amy responded I know my rights and plan to exercise them.
397. To my daughters catholic baptism I invited Zoe my spiritual advisor Silas my accountant for ten years and Rose my closest friend.
398. The committee has a no nonsense attitude even on light hearted matters.
399. My lawyers advice is to take the deal of eleven years in prison.
400. Wyatt minds his p's and q's well for a third grade student?

General Practice 2
Properly punctuate each sentence.

401. The question is this how was your weeklong trip to hawaii?
402. Well I own truth be told twelve dogs and three cats.
403. Did you add .8 ounces of vanilla extract did it taste as you hoped?
404. The flight took off at four o'clock in the morning and it landed at seven fifteen am.
405. Mia passed the midterm didn't she?
406. The question is why not?
407. I mailed the check however I forgot to sign it.
408. Ms. robinson president of PharmCo announced a stock split.
409. Speak louder please.
410. While in the big apple I stayed in a small quaint hotel near times square.
411. THE COURT we will recess for lunch until one pm.
412. The exam results won't be available for a month alex remarked.
413. Lucas wrote sophia a love poem hence he loves her.
414. Ashley my roommate forgot to set the alarm clock for five forty-five.
415. Please give the 100 page document to the bailiff ms. anderson.

416. The estimated cost to repair the bridge is between eight hundred thousand dollars and one million two hundred thousand dollars.
417. I booked the meeting room for one thirty pm and if you cancel for any reason there will be a two hundred dollar fee.
418. We selected a cute cuddly puppy from the shelter.
419. Twenty seven of every ten million factory produced toys are defective.
420. Cora lived with her sister didn't she per your prior testimony before she met and moved in with rebecca?
421. No I failed to pay the rent by five.
422. Every court reporting student needs practice time perseverance et cetera to reach the goal of writing two hundred twenty-five words per minute.
423. I like practicing to be completely honest I love capturing the spoken word.
424. Objection vague and leading.
425. Hannah loaned you twenty dollars last saturday correct?
426. I didn't want to be home alone but everyone I called didn't answer.
427. Ethan dropped his wallet somewhere have you seen it?
428. State and spell please your full name mr bell for the record.
429. After dinner last night with mrs cook margaret said I plan to move to Houston this summer.
430. I plan to move to houston said mrs cook after dinner. I have worked with my current employer since November 2015.
431. I worked fulltime for three days to reform the damaged art piece.
432. Attorneys for the plaintiff and the defendant stepped outside and argued off the record rather than on the record.
433. I packed a lunch for our day hike peanut butter sandwiches chips and bottled water.
434. Mason and ava married on january 16 2018 in seattle washington do you recall that day?
435. They gave us a verbal okay to purchase the new tires unfortunately the amount exceeded their credit limit.
436. The museum opens doesn't it at ten am on tuesdays?

437. Did you include the december january and february business purchases in the expense report?
438. Yes I did include those months in the decision making expense report.
439. No all the broad based data was not available at the time.
440. Alice said she was at work yesterday but every one I asked didn't see her.
441. While punctuating transcripts I had a light bulb moment not to dilly dally.
442. Womens clothing is more expensive than mens clothing why?
443. All right after you received the call your eta was five minutes correct?
444. My next available appointment times are monday one thirty pm, tuesday eleven thirty am, and wednesday noon.
445. Peanut butter sandwiches chips and bottled water I packed a lunch for our day hike.
446. There is a mistake in figure number 4 page thirty-seven.
447. I mailed the package on monday in fact I mailed it around noon during my lunch break.
448. My last name is spelled S a k s double i.
449. Because the discrepancy is over ten thousand dollars we prioritized it as very high.
450. Is labor day in may or september I always mix up that holiday with memorial day.

General Practice 3
Properly punctuate each sentence.

451. You can never practice too much right?
452. I can't make the appointment, I have a hearing in superior court.
453. I must clear this with the presidents secretary okay?
454. I went to the store and bought milk eggs bread.
455. I recently bought twelve apple computers for my business and I own one home.
456. I have been to the eiffel tower and while I was there I took over one hundred photographs.
457. Is it true that doctor cooper of WeCare Health examined you in july 2018?
458. I remember July 4 2016 as a cool summers day.

459. Nora witnessed the armed robbery her husband missed it because he ran into a college friend.
460. We were enjoying the movie when someone yelled fire get out.
461. Did you catch the dallas cowboys game last night?
462. I watch what people call nerd tv, shows on comic books and superheroes.
463. Admit it you returned to the scene of the crime didn't you?
464. Seventy five gallons of diesel fuel spilled on the roadway after the truck lost control and hit a tree.
465. You speak super fast, are you from the east coast?
466. Zubov vs. williams is a 1954 cook county IL patent infringement case.
467. Billy has had only one good friend since childhood Lydia.
468. Jackson countys approved budget totals two hundred fourteen million dollars.
469. Anna upon secretly paying the maître d' was immediately seated in the busy restaurant.
470. Who yelled quote/unquote fire in the packed restaurant?
471. I believe it was Mark a fifty year old man with a tatoo that covers fifty percent of his arm.
472. Melissa thought it was better to pay twenty dollars for a dozen rather than two dollars each.
473. My boss harps on the donts and neglects the dos.
474. Only three witnesses the bartender a toxicologist and a bar patron were called as witnesses by the defendants attorney.
475. Molly got on the old fashioned bus didn't she for the down town city tour?
476. She refused to agree to the contract terms unless adam did one thing apologize for his short-sighted behavior.
477. Did caleb take the wrong coat by mistake or did he take it without asking do you remember?
478. I tracked my package online as it went through nashville tennessee st. louis missouri and wichita kansas.
479. Tom how many s'es are in dessert?
480. Did your wife have your youngest daughter at home 2398 5th avenue wilwaukee WI.
481. No our daughter was born at the hospital and the doctor was doctor albert torre.

482. Unfortunately the two hour tennis match was not an action packed event.
483. Broken glass twisted metal and dripping radiator fluid debris littered the fresh crash site.
484. A woman rushed to a heavily damaged car and asked the driver are you okay?
485. The driver moaned you're an angel aren't you?
486. Scott dreamed of only thing for three consecutive nights the delivery person would finally arrive with his new steno machine.
487. When I started the car the stereo volume was on maximum but my son who last drove the car denies crankin it up.
488. The stereo speaker however was damaged and needed to be repaired unfortunately my son didn't have the money to fix it.
489. As a result, my son got a decent earning parttime job to pay the four hundred dollar repair bill.
490. Keith my son worked two months and he paid the repair bill.
491. Sadie and ava went ice skating together yet neither of them knew how to ice skate.
492. Their friends debated if ice skating was a worst case or best case situation for them.
493. Upon arriving at the ice rink they took a free beginners class.
494. The beginners class was divided into no, little, some experience groups.
495. Paul Stone junior ph.d. founded the high tech firm in 1986.
496. I can arrange a meeting with mister stone this afternoon but if you are not available I can see if mister stone can meet tomorrow at eight am.
497. Mister stone is not available tomorrow friday at 9 o'clock correct?
498. No mister stone is a friendly nice guy but his schedule is generally full.
499. Have you read the recent article, free time, in the new york times in section D, page five?
500. Yes I read and loved it you should read "25 hours a day" a book the author wrote in 2012.

Answer Key

Identifying Independent and Dependent Clauses
1. (Everyone was busy), and (I went to the movie alone).
2. (I will see) [if the book has arrived].
3. (Mary needs to check back tomorrow) [before the store opens].
4. (I'm counting calories), but (I really want dessert).
5. (Cats are good pets) [because they are clean].
6. (Tommy dragged a chair across the floor) [while his mother watched in horror].
7. (Tommy, [who is 9 years old], was scolded by his mother).
8. (I don't know) [where the keys are].
9. (Her mom was pleased) [when she got the job].
10. [As you read the textbook], (you will find the answers) [that you are looking for].
11. (The mistake [which you made] will be corrected).
12. (He ran out of money), yet (he didn't stop playing poker).
13. (I drove to school with a friend).
14. (I dove my car) [that recently got new brakes].
15. (I do not know) [how far it is to school].
16. (Mary lives one floor above you).
17. (Our secretary, [who is never late], called in sick at 9:00 a.m.)
18. (I do not know) [who gave her the flu].
19. (The client said) [that he would call us next week].
20. [When he calls], (tell him our rates have slightly increased).

Identifying Conjunctions and Transitional Expressions
21. Everyone was busy, (and) I went to the movie alone.
22. Sally didn't want to go to the dentist; [therefore], he canceled.
23. He ran out of money, (yet) he didn't stop playing poker.
24. I lost my job. [Consequently], my car got repossessed.
25. I left 30 minutes early; [however], an accident still made me late.
26. [To tell you the truth], I hate Monday mornings.
27. I saw the suspect. [In fact], I can recall what he was wearing.

Identifying Prepositional and Verbal Phrases
28. Don't step (on the broken glass).
29. [Seeing his excellent test score], he fainted.
30. The dog jump (in the car).
31. The book (on the table) is now missing.
32. [To provide a safe work environment], security cameras were installed.
33. Robert lives (in the apartment) (around the corner).
34. [Strong-minded to get the cookies (on top of the refrigerator)], Tommy dragged a chair (across the floor).

Determining Essential and Nonessential Elements
35. A man (who wore black) is the suspect.
36. Brandon, [who wore black], is the suspect.
    Note: Answer assumes element is likely nonessential.
37. The officer arrived in a black and white car, [a patrol car].
38. The defendant, [Mr. Smith], hired a private attorney.
    Note: Answer assumes there is only one defendant.
39. A psychologist (Dr. Cooper) is highly respected.
40. Amber's psychologist, [Dr. Cooper], is highly respected.
    Note: Answer assumes Amber has only one psychologist.

The Period
41. I passed the test.
42. I passed the test. We went out to dinner.
43. Please speak up.
44. Can you state and spell your full name for the record.
45. I object. The question is beyond the scope.
46. Objection. The question is vague.
47. Objection. Ambiguous. Compound.
48. Hurry. We're going to be late.
49. Damn. I don't know. Okay.
50. All right. We can take a recess now.

The Comma: Compound Sentences
51. I'm counting calories, but I really want dessert.
52. Everyone was busy, and I went to the movie alone.
53. He ran out of money, yet he didn't stop playing poker.
54. He said he was not in town yesterday, but many people saw him.
55. Linda was telling the truth, or she was telling a huge lie.

56. I lost my job last week, and my car was repossessed.
57. Tammy could not decide what to do, so she slept on it.
58. John didn't want to go to the dentist, but he went anyway.
59. I only had eight reporting jobs last month, yet I was able to pay the rent.
60. You should tell the whole story, or you will face the consequences.

The Comma: Introductory Clauses

61. To provide a safe work environment, security cameras were installed.
62. On reaching Nevada, we stopped at the first place we could gamble.
63. Running out of money, he didn't stop playing poker.
64. On the concrete sidewalk, our dog obediently sat.
65. To tell you the truth, I hate Monday mornings.
66. Across the street a squirrel darted with a nut.
    GRM: Across the street, a squirrel darted with a nut.
67. Because they are clean, cats are good pets.
68. In 2018, 91 people graduated from the small elementary school.
69. He said he was not in town yesterday. However, many people saw him.
70. While his mother watched in horror, Tommy dragged a chair across the floor.

The Comma: Nonessential Elements

71. He said he was not in town yesterday. Many people, however, saw him.
72. Mary Sue, who is my half sister, was born in 1984.
73. Did Dr. Smith, your primary care physician, see you last week?
74. I, upon arriving at the accident scene, fainted at the sight of blood.
75. It happened, you know, right after, like, dinner.
76. The tree, tall and strong, withstood the strong winds.
77. The motion, filed just yesterday, was immediately denied by the judge.
78. I don't like the looks of this, to tell you the truth.
79. Dr. Jones, of WeCare Health, is my physical therapist.
80. My situation, in so many words, is bad.

The Comma: Series of Items
81. I need to buy milk and bread.
82. I need to buy milk, eggs, and bread.
83. I need to buy milk, eggs, bread.
84. I need to buy milk and eggs and bread.
85. Please invite John, Sue, Jill, and Sarah to the meeting.
86. A court reporting student needs a steno machine, a computer, the textbooks, et cetera.
87. A court reporting student needs to buy the textbook, the workbook, a notebook, et cetera, before the first day of instruction.
88. Did you mail the invitations and response cards and directions to the guests?
89. Did you mail the invitations, response cards, and directions to the guests?
90. Did you mail the invitations, response cards, et cetera, to the guests?

The Comma: Coordinate Adjectives
91. It will be another hot, windy day.
92. His cruel, callous actions demanded a severe sentence.
93. The old ghost town is not on the map.
94. The smart, charismatic employee quickly promoted to shift manager.

The Comma: Miscellaneous
95. Please approach the bench, Ms. Anderson.
96. I briskly walk, never jog, one hour each day.
97. Did you invite Melody Jones, Esq., to the briefing?
98. Mr. Davies Jr. is also attending the briefing.
      BPPG: "Mr. Davis, Jr., is . . ."
99. Explain what you mean, sir, by "gently used"?
100. The policy in question is Section 4, paragraph 12.
101. The attorneys conferred off the record, not on the record.
102. Mr. Jones III died last week after a long illness.
103. Did you know Mr. Jones Sr. founded the law firm?
      BGGP: ". . . Mr. Jones, Sr., founded . . ."
104. I am quoting from page 103, line 9.
105. Please speak up, sir.

The Semicolon: Compound Sentences

106. My father's ancestors are from Germany; my mother's ancestors are from England.
107. I saw James in the corner of my eye; unfortunately, I did not see which direction he went.
108. I did my homework; however, I did the wrong set of problems.
109. Ashley was the only person who could make the decision; therefore, she weighed the evidence carefully.
110. She weighed the evidence; as a result, the decision was sound.
111. Please schedule the deposition for Monday; or if you prefer, we can do it Tuesday.
112. Richard does not like broccoli; in other words, he hates it.
113. Her daughter loves broccoli; and if you can believe this, she asks for more.
114. I told the truth; as I see it, I told the whole truth.
115. I like him; to be honest, I love him.
116. I scheduled the car repair for this afternoon; or in the event you're unavailable, I can reschedule for another day.
117. I saw the accident; my husband saw nothing.
118. I saw the accident; needless to say, my husband saw nothing.
119. I saw James in the corner of my eye; thus I did not see which direction he went.
120. I saw James in the corner of my eye; notwithstanding, I did not see which direction he went.
121. I saw James in the corner of my eye; and as a result, I did not see which direction he went.
122. Jack loves Melissa; in fact, he sent her flowers.
123. Jack sent Melissa flowers; obviously, he loves her.
124. Jack sent Melissa flowers; hence he loves her.
125. Jack sent Melissa flowers; however, he forgot the card.

The Semicolon: Series of Items

126. Please grab the red ring of keys, the car keys; a bottle of water from the refrigerator; and my lunch.
127. I arrived at work at 9:30 a.m.; turned on my computer; and called Denise, the director's secretary.

128. The defendant has lived in New York City, New York; San Francisco, California; and Detroit, Michigan.
129. The reasons for the employment termination were, first, excessive tardiness; second, substandard work quality; and, third, arguing with other employees.
130. I invited Jim, the office manager; Joan, the financial manager; and Linda, the supervisor, to the annual budget meeting.
131. The officer stated that he contacted the people living at the address of the complaint given five minutes earlier by dispatch; that he talked to the people living at the address about the recent noise complaint of the party; and that he advised the people living at the address to turn down the volume on the large stereo system.
132. My next available times are Wednesday, 9:00 a.m.; Thursday, 1:30 p.m.; and Friday, 10:30 a.m.
133. I quit my last job because, one, the manager was verbally abusive; two, better pay; and, three, better benefits.
134. The account payments were received on June 9, 2017; July 11, 2017; August 6, 2017; and September 10, 2017.
135. I consulted with my lawyer, Ms. Anderson; my CPA, Mr. Smith; and an expert in the field, Ms. Cooper.

The Colon

136. Luke did not know a new law: All bicyclists must wear helmets.

    Note: A period or semicolon could be used in place of the colon.
137. Amy is only afraid of one bug: spiders.
138. He had his favorite meal when dining out: soup, steak, and French fries.
139. The following law enforcement agencies were at the scene of the accident: a sheriff, an NYPD officer, and a detective.
140. The accident report contained one glaring fact: He was traveling well above the speed limit based on the skid marks.

    Note: A period or semicolon could be used in place of the colon.

141. An attorney advised me about my claim: There was probably not enough evidence to win in court.
Note: A period or semicolon could be used in place of the colon.
142. THE COURT: Juror No. 5 is dismissed.
143. Susan passed the skills test: Her endless hours of practice paid off.
Note: A period or semicolon could be used in place of the colon.
144. These are the reasons for the increase in Bay Area home sales: economic recovery and low-interest rates.
145. I want you to understand that I saw a large, hairy thing that night: a Bigfoot.
146. Several vehicles were involved in the accident: a passenger car, a semi, and a pickup truck.
147. MRS. ANDERSON: The witness has not been qualified as an expert.
148. John failed to make the job candidate list: He was just shy of the experience requirement.
Note: A period or semicolon could be used in place of the colon.
149. She had only one thought on her mind after rushing to get ready for work: Did she turn the iron off?
150. We know your reason for the murder: money.

The Dash
151. I took -- borrowed the money.
152. I'll be frank with you -- mark my words because this is the honest truth -- I did not steal the money.
153. Q   Did you steal --
     A   No.
     Q   -- the money?
154. Q   How long did it take you to recover --
     A   Four months.
     Q   -- from the surgery?
155. The primary defense team -- Tom, Sue, and I -- was retained on April 2, 2018.
156. The needed food -- bread, milk, and cheese -- was bought on the way home.
157. Tom, Sue, and I -- the primary defense team was retained on April 2, 2018.

158. Bread, milk, and cheese -- the needed food was bought on the way home.
159. Q Were you speeding --
    A Can we take a break?
    Q   After this question. -- at the time of the accident?
      GRM: After this question -- at the time of the accident?
160. Jackie, James, and Joan -- each will be speaking at the annual company dinner.

The Question Mark: Echo and Non-Echo Questions
161. She's right, isn't she?
162. He proposed to you Saturday evening, didn't he?
163. There were two suspects, wasn't there, in the vehicle?
164. The children were excited, were they not, that Christmas morning?
165. You were headed southbound -- is that correct? -- during the evening commute?
166. There were two suspects – wasn't there to your knowledge -- in the vehicle?
167. You were headed southbound? Is that a good statement?
168. The defendant wore a blue jacket. Do you recall?
169. You were headed southbound. Isn't that correct?
    LMEG: Use a period with a semicolon optional.
    BGGP: Use a semicolon.
    GRM: Use a comma. A period or semicolon is acceptable.
170. She drove, didn't she, southbound?
171. You have never lived in a big city, have you?
172. I'm right, am I not, that you've only lived out in the country?
173. You have only lived out in the country, right?
    LMEG: Before "right," use a period with a semicolon or comma optional.
    BGGP: Before "right," a use semicolon.
    GRM: Before "right," use a comma. A period or semicolon is acceptable.
174. You were headed southbound. Do you remember?

The Question Mark:
Questions with "To Be" and Connected Questions
175. What I asked was, Did you date the plaintiff in 2017?

    BGGP: What I asked was did you date the plaintiff in 2017?

176. The question is why not?

177. Was his coat red? White? Blue?

    LMEG, BGGP, and GRM allow: Was his coat red? white? blue?

178. The question is this: How is your father doing after his hip replacement?

179. What I asked was how much?

180. My last question was, You saw Dr. Cooper on January 11, 2018?

    BGGP: My last question was you saw Dr. Cooper on January 11, 2018?

The Quotation Mark and Italics: Punctuation Marks
181. Freddie screamed, "fire."

182. "Let's go out for dinner," Rory said.

183. Linda turned the TV to a "nature show": a shark feeding frenzy.

184. Tom said, "grab one"; "grab what," Mindy responded.

185. Susan asked, "Are you feeling lucky today?"

186. "I'm flying to Detroit," Tom signed. "You go where the work is."

The Quotation Mark and Italics: Direct Quotations
187. The officer said, "Drop it."

188. She replied, "I'm going to quit this job if I don't get a raise."

189. James said, "I'll drop it off on my way home."

190. "Put your hands on your head," the officer instructed.

191. "I got the job," I squealed.

192. The report says, "At 3:17 p.m., a stolen-car call was received."

193. The code section states, "All persons shall give a notice of 30 days."

194. "Don't hit your brother," Tammy said sternly. "You must learn to share."

195. "I'm going to quit this job," she replied, "if I don't get a raise."

196. Rachel asked, "What do you want for dinner tonight?"
197. Did Rachel ask, "What do you want for dinner tonight?"
198. Did Angela say, "I'm making spaghetti for dinner"?
199. The officer said, quote, "Drop it," unquote.
     LMEG: The officer said, quote, Drop it, unquote.
     LMEG: The officer said, "Drop it."
200. William replied, quote/unquote, "I quit."
     LMEG: William replied, quote/unquote, I quit.
     LMEG: William replied, "I quit."
201. The code section states, quote, "All persons shall give a notice of 30 days."
     LMEG: The code section states, quote, All persons shall give a notice of 30 days.
     LMEG: The code section states, "All persons shall give a notice of 30 days."
202. The report stated the important detail on page 3: "At 3:17 p.m., a stolen-car call was received."
203. The officer was forceful in his instructions: "Drop it."
204. Peter said, "I don't understand these detailed instructions."
205. Amy responded, "I know the laws in this state."
206. "I could not tell you," Tim responded, "what Andrew's problem is."
207. "The tax on the car is over $3,000," Randy gasped.
208. I think the suspect said, quote, "Give me your wallet," close quote.
     LMEG: I think the suspect said, quote, Give me your wallet, close quote.
     LMEG: I think the suspect said, "Give me your wallet."
209. Did the suspect say, quote/unquote, "Give me your wallet"?
     LMEG: Did the suspect say, quote/unquote, Give me your wallet?
     LMEG: Did the suspect say, "Give me your wallet"?
210. Deborah asked, "How much did it cost to fix the car?"

The Quotation Mark and Italics:
Titles, Special Emphasis, and Definitions
211. The book chapter is titled "Know Your Punctuation."
212. Ann's favorite *Home and Garden* TV show episode is "Backyard Décor."
213. Due to Jack's previous jail escape, he is termed "high risk."
214. Mr. Wright said he bought a "chopper," a gun, while on parole.
215. In *Roberts v. Pharmco*, the plaintiff claimed fraud.
216. Have you seen the *Star Trek* episode "The Enemy Within"?
217. What did Mr. Smith, the defendant, mean by "self-help"?
218. For your question, I recommend reading the chapter titled "The New You" in the bestseller *Be Your Best*.
219. The movie accurately captured the *zeitgeist* of the late 1970s.
220. The dictionary defines *zeitgeist* as "the general intellectual, moral, and cultural climate of an era."

Capitalization
221. Ward Stone Ireland invented the Stenotype.
222. Main Street and First Street do not intersect.
223. Have you read *The History of Court Reporting in the 1970s*?
224. Did I leave my copy of *Punctuation for Proofreaders* on the table?
225. Did you see Captain James Roller at the VFW meeting?
226. Did James Roller, captain of the 103rd Infantry Division, attend the VFW meeting?
227. Ted Cruz, Senator from Texas, attended the heated public hearing?
228. Did you visit your mom during Christmas vacation?
229. I can't believe Dad said he was not coming for Easter dinner.
230. Is it true, Detective, that you found a bloody knife in the trash?
231. The officer pursued the suspect's car south on Elm Street.
232. That's a distinctive accent. Were you born in the South?

233. Yes, I was born in New Orleans near the French Quarter.
234. The Golden Gate Bridge is in the Bay Area.
235. The Empire State Building is in the Big Apple.
236. The headquarters of Intel is in Silicon Valley.
237. The Hoover City Council meets Wednesdays.
238. I live in the city of Sacramento.
239. I got a parking ticket from the City of Sacramento.
240. Last June, I filed a claim in Hoover County Superior Court.
241. Eve filed a court case that summer.
242. The best time to buy a Toyota Prius is in January.
243. The worst time to buy a Dodge truck is in July.
244. Is Tylenol or ibuprofen better for a toothache?
245. I lived with a roommate who insisted on using Charmin toilet paper.
246. Does New Year's Eve fall on a Wednesday or Thursday this year?
247. Does the defendant understand English or Spanish?
248. The suspect was described as either Hispanic or Caucasian.
249. The victim was sitting on a park bench reading the Qur'an.
250. The victim is an atheist and does not believe in a god.

Numbers: Writing Numbers and Figures
251. I only have three pairs of tennis shoes.
252. I have over 100 books in my personal library.
253. Was Linda 8 years old when her parents divorced?
254. Amanda owns 14 vintage cars.
255. Do you really own 11 dogs and 2 cats?
256. No, I two dogs and nine cats.
257. The population in Oregon in 1973 was 2.2 million.
258. Is the 1973 Oregon population found on page 1103 of the transcript?
259. The U.S. national debt is expected to exceed $24 trillion this year.
260. Is the city project estimated at $775,000 or $1,100,000?
261. Three squirrels ran across the road
262. Twenty-five out of the 4,500 ballots were received.
263. 203 small earthquakes were recorded in California last year.

264. 109 new bird species were cataloged in the last 12 years.
265. 1U is the apartment number.

Numbers: Time and Dates
266. The accident occurred on June 5, 2016.
267. Did the accident occur on 5 June 2016?
268. Sue's birthday is August 23, 1995.
269. Her younger brother's birthday is October 11, 1998.
270. The accident occurred on June 5, 2016, along Hillsdale Drive.
271. The accident occurred on 5 June 2016 along Hillsdale Drive
272. The accident occurred in June 2016 along Hillsdale Drive.

273. I left work at 5:00 p.m.
    Alternate: 5 p.m.
274. I left work at 1700 hours.
275. I set my alarm clock for 6:15.
276. I set my alarm clock for 0600 hours.
277. The morning commute traffic starts at six o'clock.
    BGGP: 6:00 o'clock
278. I leave for work at five o'clock when it's still dark.
    BGGP: 5:00 o'clock
279. The accident occurred on June 5, 2016, at about 7:30 in the morning.
280. The accident occurred in June 2016 at about seven o'clock in the morning.
    BGGP: 7:00 o'clock

Numbers: Money
281. The car repair bill totaled about $600.
282. Wow, I only paid $450 for the same repair at my shop.
283. Did Amy give you a $20 bill?
284. No, Amy handed me $10.25.
285. What happened to the other 75 cents?
286. She bought a candy bar for $.75 and gave me $10.25.
287. Did Tim buy that motorcycle for $10,000?
288. No, he bought it for 8,000.
289. What did Tim do with the spare $2,000?
290. He purchased new tires for 300 or 400 dollars.

291. Tim also repaid his mom $200.
292. For every returned check, there is a $29.95 fee.
293. Did you see the soup on sale for 99 cents each?
294. Yes, that's a savings of about $1.50 each.
295. Buy a dozen and save $18.

Numbers: Miscellaneous
296. My mailing address is 1313 55th Avenue, Woodside, California 94062.
297. My previous address was One Mills Street.
298. I bought 8 acres of my parents' property or 10 percent of what they own.
299. My height is 6 feet 2 inches; my brother is six-three.
      BGGP: six three or 6-3
      GRM: six, three
300. The new law needs a two-thirds majority to pass.
301. Five-eighths of students need financial aid.
302. The cut was 3/32 of an inch deep.
303. The manufacturing process is described on page 23, Figure 2.
304. The second step in the chemistry experiment is to add 0.3 ounces of water.
305. I was born in the 1990s
      BGGP: 1990s or 1990's.

Abbreviation
306. The U.S. national debt per taxpayer is $180,000.
      LMEG, BGGP, GRM: U.S.
      MW: US or U.S.
307. The Greek Battle of Marathon occurred in 490 B.C.
      LMEG, BGGP, GRM: B.C.
      MW: BC
308. Is it true, Dr. Cooper, that you failed to perform a complete examination?
309. How many local CEOs attended the city budget meeting?
310. Dr. Bell, D.D.S., has been my dentist for nearly 20 years.
      LMEG, BGGP, GRM: D.D.S.
      MW: DDS
311. The report states, "approximate vehicle speed: 45 mph."

312. Ms. Anderson, CEO, married Mr. Smith Sr., Ph.D.
     <u>LMEG, BGGP, GRM</u>: Ph.D.
     <u>MW</u>: PhD
313. How many TVs do you have in your home?
     <u>BGGP</u>: TVs or TV's
314. Okay. Did you steal the money, jewelry, et cetera?
315. I told the 911 operator to come ASAP.

Apostrophe
316. Someone stole the plaintiff's purse from the courtroom.
317. Tom claimed the heavy lifting violated workers' rights.
318. April's wallet is missing. Have you seen it?
319. Children's toys are so expensive.
320. Frank's testimony did not help the case.
321. I want to hear the next two witnesses' testimony.
322. I bought some fresh produce at the farmers' market.
323. How do you think the girls' soccer team will do this year?
324. Don't use the boys restroom by mistake.
325. Is there one or two I's in traveled?
326. Each judge has their do's and don'ts
     <u>MW</u>: dos and don'ts
327. I spell my name, Bret, with one t, not two t's.
328. I sold my '68 Ford Mustang.
329. I don't recall. My last surgery was in either 2017 or '18.
330. Did you say "talkin'" or "walkin'"?
331. Cindy x'd out the spelling mistake and wrote the correction above.
332. Patrick ID'd the suspect who was handcuffed in the patrol car.
333. I 86'd the junk straight into the trashcan.
334. I need to get my boss's approval.
335. I gave my two weeks' notice at work

The Hyphen: General
336. Who won the countywide race in district 2?
337. Were there any postoperative complications?
338. The illegal firearms found in the raid consisted mostly of semiautomatic rifles.
339. The witness corrected his statement and re-marked the exhibit.

340. I lived on a small co-op until 14 years old.
341. Do you have and post-Thanksgiving traditions?
342. Is your position at the law firm full-time or part-time?
343. The X-ray technician x-rayed my arm in four different angles or positions.
    <u>MW</u>: see above
    <u>LMEG</u>: X-ray technician and X-rayed
    <u>BGGP</u>: x-ray technician and x-rayed
344. I invest in both long- and short-term securities.
345. On Tuesdays, the board has an open- and closed-door session.
346. Focus groups were divided into 20-, 30-, and 40-year-olds.
347. As I recall, I had a hotel room on the twenty-second or -third floor.
348. My last name is Schmidt S-c-h-m-i-d-t, not Smith.
349. My name is Staci Green S-t-a-c-i G-r, double e, -n.

The Hyphen: Compound Words
350. I once saw a group of zookeepers capture a man-eating alligator.
351. The required typing exam for the job was a pass-fail test.
352. Are there any cross-references for the compound adjective rules in the *Chicago Manual of Style*?
353. Please check the timetable to see what time the bus arrives.
354. I was shortchanged by the cashier.
355. Did you have your suit dry-cleaned before the start of the trial?
356. A high-level meeting was scheduled after the annual budget was not approved.
357. I feared a worst-case situation: layoffs.
358. However, the bottom-line results were no raises or overtime.
359. This caused a year of penny-pinching purchases and decisions.
360. I hope the budget crisis is not a long-lasting problem.
361. What stopped me cold was the "are you seriously that freaking stupid" look.

362. The fast-paced and lopsided football game ended in our favor.
363. The newly formed football team needed more practice.
364. I received a "how you doing after all these years?" welcome.
365. The old coal-mining town is a popular hiking destination.

Yes and No
366. Yes, I do.
367. I do not, no.
368. I work for the County of Santa Clara. No.
369. Yes. She left with James around 4:30 p.m.
370. I worked until 5:00 p.m. that day. No.
371. No, I did not see her leave.
372. No, I was not speeding.
373. No. I was driving about 35 miles per hour.
374. The posted speed limit is 35. No.
375. No, I wasn't.

General Practice 1
376. Logan suddenly left his job because, one, poor pay; two, poor management; and, three, long commute.
377. I left my trash cans out too long and got a $50 fine from the City of Burlingame.
378. Isabella passed the final speed test. She and her boyfriend went out to dinner.
     Alternate: "…test; she…"
379. I saw the car in the corner of my eye at the last second. Unfortunately, I was unable to avoid the collision
     Alternate: "…second; unfortunately…"
380. Did Liam ask, "What shall we do tonight for dinner?"
381. The suspect in the police lineup was ID'd by Emma.
382. The crack in the windshield measured 7/16 of an inch across.
383. According to our records, the date of loss is September 5, 2018.
384. The detained teens included a 13-, 15-, and17-year-old.
385. I can't believe Jackson likes cooked carrots; and if you can believe this, he also likes other vegetables.

386. Sophia was tardy -- wasn't she to the best of your knowledge -- to work each day?
387. Punctuation mastery is a lifelong journey.
388. My mother called my about the situation: The water heater stopped working, and there is no hot water.
   Alternate: "...situation. The..."
   Alternate: "...situation; the..."
389. Did Mr. Pearson file a claim in Lake County Superior Court?
390. Did you sell your classic '57 Chevy at the car auction in May 2017?
391. I took aspirin for my headache. Isn't Tylenol better?
392. The probation officer reported that he contacted a male and female living at the recently added address in the old case file; that the couple stated they are renters who had moved into the home in either June or July of 2018; and that James had not stopped by to see them or been seen in the area for a long time.
393. The poorly constructed wood deck cost me $5,000 to remove and rebuild.
394. I bought several tomato sauce cans for $.60 each and saved $2.
395. Riley Walker, lieutenant in the Salvation Army, helped organize the winter clothing drive.
396. Amy responded, "I know my rights and plan to exercise them."
397. To my daughter's Catholic baptism, I invited Zoe, my spiritual advisor; Silas, my accountant for ten years; and Rose, my closest friend.
398. The committee has a no-nonsense attitude even on lighthearted matters.
399. My lawyer's advice is to take the deal of 11 years in prison.
400. Wyatt minds his p's and q's well for a third-grade student.

General Practice 2
401. The question is this: How was your weeklong trip to Hawaii?
402. Well, I own, truth be told, 12 dogs and 3 cats.
403. Did you add 0.8 ounces of vanilla extract? Did it taste as you hoped?

404. The flight took off at four o'clock in the morning, and it landed at 7:15 a.m.
    BGGP: 4:00 o'clock
405. Mia passed the midterm, didn't she?
406. The question is why not?
407. I mailed the check. However, I forgot to sign it.
    Alternate: ". . . check; however, . . ."
408. Ms. Robinson, president of PharmCo, announced a stock split.
409. Speak louder, please.
410. While in the Big Apple, I stayed in a small, quaint hotel near Times Square.
411. THE COURT: We will recess for lunch until 1:00 p.m.
    Alternate: 1 p.m.
412. "The exam results won't be available for a month," Alex remarked.
413. Lucas wrote Sophia a love poem. Hence he loves her.
    Alternate: ". . . poem; hence . . ."
414. Ashley, my roommate, forgot to set the alarm clock for 5:45.
415. Please give the 100-page document to the bailiff, Ms. Anderson.
416. The estimated cost to repair the bridge is between $800,000 and $1,200,000.
417. I booked the meeting room for 1:30 p.m.; and if you cancel for any reason, there will be a $200 fee.
418. We selected a cute, cuddly puppy from the shelter.
419. Twenty-seven of every 10 million factory-produced toys are defective.
420. Cora lived with her sister -- didn't she per your prior testimony -- before she met and moved in with Rebecca?
421. No, I failed to pay the rent by 5:00.
    Alternate: five
422. Every court reporting student needs practice time, perseverance, et cetera, to reach the goal of writing 225 words per minute.
423. I like practicing. To be completely honest, I love capturing the spoken word.
    Alternate: ". . . practicing; to be . . ."
424. Objection. Vague and leading.

425. Hannah loaned you $20 last Saturday. Correct?
    <u>LMEG</u>: Before "correct," use a period with a semicolon or comma optional.
    <u>BGGP</u>: Before "correct," use a semicolon.
    <u>GRM</u>: Before "correct," use a comma. A period or semicolon is acceptable.
426. I didn't want to be home alone, but everyone I called didn't answer.
427. Ethan dropped his wallet somewhere. Have you seen it?
428. State and spell, please, your full name, Mr. Bell, for the record.
429. After dinner last night with Mrs. Cook, Margaret said, "I plan to move to Houston this summer."
430. "I plan to move to Houston," said Mrs. Cook after dinner. "I have worked with my current employer since November 2015."
431. I worked full-time for three days to re-form the damaged art piece.
432. Attorneys for the plaintiff and the defendant stepped outside and argued off the record, rather than on the record.
433. I packed a lunch for our day hike: peanut butter sandwiches, chips, and bottled water.
434. Mason and Ava married on January 16, 2018, in Seattle, Washington. Do you recall that day?
435. They gave us a verbal okay to purchase the new tires. Unfortunately, the amount exceeded their credit limit.
    <u>Alternate</u>: ". . . tires; unfortunately, . . ."
436. The museum opens, doesn't it, at 10:00 a.m. on Tuesdays?
437. Did you include the December, January, and February business purchases in the expense report?
438. Yes, I did include those months in the decision-making expense report.
439. No, all the broad-based data was not available at the time.
440. Alice said she was at work yesterday, but everyone I asked didn't see her.
441. While punctuating transcripts, I had a lightbulb moment not to dillydally.

442. Women's clothing is more expensive than men's clothing. Why?

443. All right. After you received the call, your ETA was 5 minutes. Right?
    LMEG: Before "right," use a period with a semicolon or comma optional.
    BGGP: Before "right," use a semicolon.
    GRM: Before "right," use a comma. A period or semicolon is acceptable.

444. My next available appointment times are Monday, 1:30 p.m.; Tuesday, 11:30 a.m.; and Wednesday, noon.

445. Peanut butter sandwiches, chips, and bottled water -- I packed a lunch for our day hike.

446. There is a mistake in Figure No.4, page 37.

447. I mailed the package on Monday. In fact, I mailed it around noon during my lunch break.
    Alternate: ". . . Monday; in fact, . . ."

448. My last name is spelled S-a-k-s, double i.

449. Because the discrepancy is over $10,000, we prioritized it as "very high."

450. Is Labor Day in May or September? I always mix up that holiday with Memorial Day.

General Practice 3

451. You can never practice too much. Right?
    LMEG: Before "right," use a period with a semicolon or comma optional.
    BGGP: Before "right," use a semicolon.
    GRM: Before "right," use a comma. A period or semicolon is acceptable.

452. I can't make the appointment. I have a hearing in superior court.
    Alternate: ". . . appointment; I . . ."

453. I must clear this with the president's secretary. Okay?

454. I went to the store and bought milk, eggs, bread.

455. I recently bought 12 Apple computers for my business, and I own one home.

456. I have been to the Eiffel Tower; and while I was there, I took over 100 photographs.

457. Is it true that Dr. Cooper, of WeCare Health, examined you in July 2018?
458. I remember July 4, 2016, as a cool summer's day.
459. Nora witnessed the armed robbery. Her husband missed it because he ran into a college friend.
    Alternate: ". . . robbery; her . . ."
460. We were enjoying the movie when someone yelled, "Fire. Get out."
461. Did you catch the Dallas Cowboys game last night?
462. I watch what people call "nerd TV": shows on comic books and superheroes.
463. Admit it. You returned to the scene of the crime, didn't you?
464. Seventy-five gallons of diesel fuel spilled on the roadway after the truck lost control and hit a tree.
465. You speak super fast. Are you from the East Coast?
466. *Zubov v. Williams* is a 1954 Cook County, Illinois, patent infringement case.
467. Billy has had only one good friend since childhood: Lydia.
468. Jackson County's approved budget totals $214 million.
469. Anna, upon secretly paying the maître d', was immediately seated in the busy restaurant.
470. Who yelled, quote/unquote, "Fire," in the packed restaurant?
    LMEG: Who yelled, quote/unquote, Fire, in the packed restaurant?
    LMEG: Who yelled, "Fire," in the packed restaurant?
471. I believe it was Mark, a 50-year-old man with a tattoo that covers 50 percent of his arm.
472. Melissa thought it was better to pay $20 for a dozen, rather than $2 each.
473. My boss harps on the don'ts and neglects the do's.
474. Only three witnesses -- the bartender, a toxicologist, and a bar patron -- were called as witnesses by the defendant's attorney.
475. Molly got on the old-fashioned bus, didn't she, for the downtown city tour?
476. She refused to agree to the contract terms unless Adam did one thing: apologize for his short-sighted behavior.

477. Did Caleb take the wrong coat by mistake, or did he take it without asking? Do you remember?
478. I tracked my package online as it went through Nashville, Tennessee; St. Louis, Missouri; and Wichita, Kansas.
479. Tom, how many s's are in dessert?
480. Did your wife have your youngest daughter at home: 2398 Fifth Avenue, Milwaukee, Wisconsin.
481. No. Our daughter was born at the hospital, and the doctor was Dr. Albert Torre.
482. Unfortunately, the two-hour tennis match was not an action-packed event.
483. Broken glass, twisted metal, and dripping radiator fluid -- debris littered the fresh crash site.
484. A woman rushed to a heavily damaged car and asked the driver, "Are you okay?"
485. The driver moaned, "You're an angel, aren't you?"
486. Scott dreamed of only thing for three consecutive nights: The delivery person would finally arrive with his new steno machine.
     Alternate: ". . . nights. The . . ."
     Alternate: ". . . nights; the . . ."
487. When I started the car, the stereo volume was on maximum; but my son who last drove the car denies "crankin' it up."
488. The stereo speaker, however, was damaged and needed to be repaired. Unfortunately, my son didn't have the money to fix it.
     Alternate: ". . . repaired; unfortunately, . . ."
489. As a result, my son got a decent-earning, part-time job to pay the $400 repair bill.
490. Keith, my son, worked two months; and he paid the repair bill.
491. Sadie and Ava went ice skating together, yet neither of them knew how to ice skate.
492. Their friends debated if ice skating was a worst-case or best-case situation for them.
493. Upon arriving at the ice rink, they took a free beginners' class.

494. The beginners' class was divided into no-, little-, some-experience groups.
495. Paul Stone Jr., Ph.D., founded the hi-tech firm in 1986.
496. I can arrange a meeting with Mr. Stone this afternoon; but if you are not available, I can see if Mr. Stone can meet tomorrow at 8:00 a.m.
497. Mr. Stone is not available tomorrow, Friday, at nine o'clock. Correct?
    LMEG: Before "correct," a use period with a semicolon or comma optional.
    BGGP: Before "correct," use a semicolon.
    GRM: Before "correct," use a comma. A period or semicolon is acceptable.
    BGGP: 9:00 o'clock
498. No. Mr. Stone is a friendly, nice guy, but his schedule is generally full.
499. Have you read the recent article "Free Time" in the *New York Times* in Section D, page 5?
500. Yes, I read and loved it. You should read *25 Hours a Day*, a book the author wrote in 2012.